JOURNAL

PETER PAUPER PRESS, INC.
WHITE PLAINS, NEW YORK

PETER PAUPER PRESS
Fine Books and Gifts Since 1928

Our Company

In 1928, at the age of twenty-two, Peter Beilenson began printing books on a small press in the basement of his parents' home in Larchmont, New York. Peter—and later his wife, Edna—sought to create fine books that sold at "prices even a pauper could afford."

Today, still family owned and operated, Peter Pauper Press continues to honor our founders' legacy—and our customers' expectations—of beauty, quality, and value.

Cover art copyright © The British Library Board / C.109.p.20
This journal's opulent cover design reproduces a jeweled, gold-tooled goatskin binding created in London in 1905.

Designed by Margaret Rubiano

Copyright © 2013
Peter Pauper Press, Inc.
202 Mamaroneck Avenue
White Plains, NY 10601
All rights reserved
ISBN 978-1-4413-1224-2
Printed in China
7 6 5 4

Visit us at www.peterpauper.com